FAR OUT!

The Chemistry of **Space**

Written by William D. Adams

WORLD BOOK

www.worldbook.com

Co-published by agreement between Shi Tu Hui and World Book, Inc.

Shi Tu Hui
Room 1807, Block 1,
#3 West Dawang Road
Chaoyang District, Beijing 100025
P.R. China

World Book, Inc.
180 North LaSalle Street
Suite 900
Chicago, Illinois 60601
USA

© 2026. All rights reserved. This volume may not be reproduced in whole or in part in any form without prior written permission from the publisher.

WORLD BOOK and the GLOBE DEVICE are registered trademarks or trademarks of World Book, Inc.

Library of Congress Control Number: 2025942241

Aha! Academy: Chemistry
ISBN: 978-0-7166-7346-0 (set, hardcover)

Far Out! The Chemistry of Space
ISBN: 978-0-7166-7354-5 (hard cover)
ISBN: 978-0-7166-7374-3 (e-book)
ISBN: 978-0-7166-7364-4 (soft cover)

Staff

Editorial

Vice President
Tom Evans

Senior Manager, New Content
Jeff De La Rosa

Senior Curriculum Designer
Caroline Davidson

Curriculum Designer
Mikayla Kightlinger

Content Creator
Joseph P. Cataliotti

Proofreader
Nathalie Strassheim

Indexer
Nathaniel Lindstrom

Graphics and Design

Senior Visual Communications Designer
Melanie Bender

Designer
Shannon Hagman

Written by William D. Adams

Designed by Starletta Polster

Acknowledgments

The publishers gratefully acknowledge the following sources for photography. All illustrations were prepared by WORLD BOOK unless otherwise noted.

Cover: Alones/Shutterstock; Aphelleon/Shutterstock; Inozemtsev Konstantin/Shutterstock; IrenaR/Shutterstock; Nazarii_Neshcherenskyi/Shutterstock

Album/Alamy 7; © Galaxy Picture Library/Alamy 19; © History and Art Collection/Alamy 15; © J Marshall - Tribaleye Images/Alamy 23; © NC Collections/Alamy 39; © NASA Image Collection/Alamy 4; © Science Photo Library/Alamy 37; © Science History Images/Alamy 11; NASA 4, 5, 9, 13, 17, 18, 19, 21, 26, 27, 28, 30, 31, 32, 33, 34, 35, 36, 37, 41, 42, 43, 46, 47; NOAA 28; © Shutterstock 3, 5, 6, 7, 8, 9, 10, 11, 12, 13, 14, 15, 16, 17, 19, 20, 21, 22, 23, 24, 25, 26, 27, 28, 29, 30, 31, 32, 33, 35, 36, 38, 39, 40, 41, 42, 43, 44, 45, 46, 47, 48; © WORLD BOOK diagram by Precision Graphics 40

There is a glossary of terms on page 48. Terms defined in the glossary are in type that looks like *this* on their first appearance on any spread (two facing pages).

Contents

Introduction 4

① **Star-studded chemistry** 6
    Stellar lives 8
    Vital element: helium 10
    Supergiants and supernovas. 12

② **Closer to home** 14
    The windy sun 16
    The moon rocks 18
    Solar system snowballs 20
    Studying space rocks 22
    Impact-ful chemistry 24
    Gas giants 26
    Looking for life 28
    Earth's evil twin 30
    The Red Planet 32
    Titan-ic chemistry .34
    Frozen worlds 36

③ **Exploring space** 38
    Getting to space 40
    Living in space 42

Build a rocket 44
Index 46
Glossary 48

Introduction

Have you ever wondered what the stars are made of or how planets form? The answers to these questions can be discovered through the chemistry of space!

In this book, we'll take an exciting journey beyond Earth to discover chemistry throughout the cosmos. We'll explore how various chemical elements work together to create everything from stars to asteroids. You'll learn how stars "cook" new elements deep in their cores and how those elements spread across space when stars explode. We'll also discover the chemistry of our solar system, including chemical wonders in the rings of Saturn, the icy comets, and the *atmospheres* of distant planets. Then, chemistry will help us tackle the biggest question in astronomy—Is there life out there, and how do we find it? Finally, we'll study the chemistry that enables us to get into space and keep intrepid astronauts alive, healthy, and happy far from Earth.

This book will give you a whole new way to look at the universe. Ready for liftoff? Let's explore the chemistry of space!

1 STAR-STUDDED CHEMISTRY

Stars are the elemental factories of the universe. They take the vast amounts of hydrogen created in the big bang and churn out all the other elements of the periodic table.

Even the largest stars form from tiny particles called atoms. Atoms are made up of three subatomic particles: positively charged protons, negatively charged electrons, and neutrons, which have a neutral charge. Protons and neutrons clump together to form the atomic nucleus (core). Electrons don't stick to the nucleus, but instead tend to be found in the area around it.

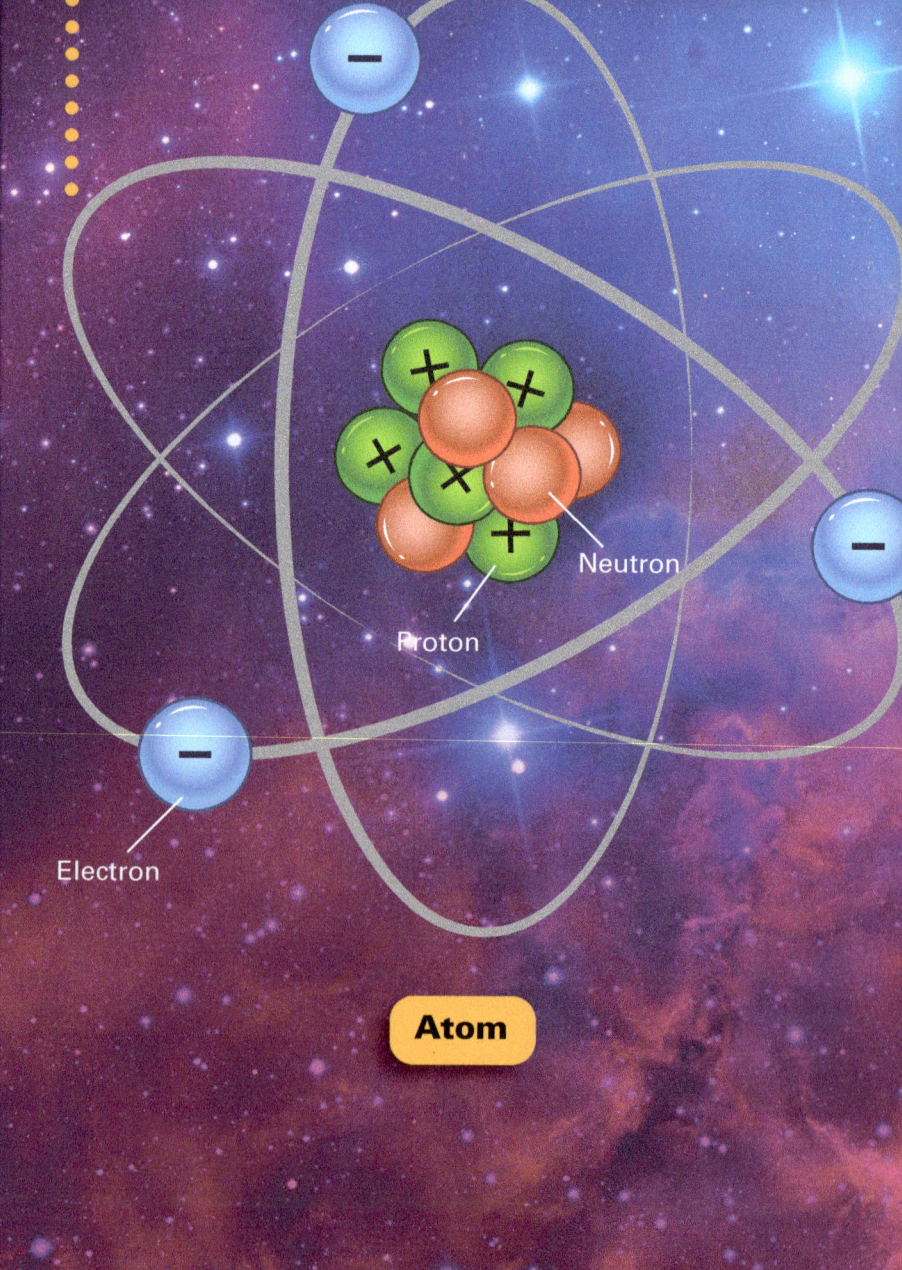

Atom

One chemical element is the most common in the universe—hydrogen. Hydrogen is the simplest possible atom, consisting of just one proton and one electron. Some *isotopes* (forms) of hydrogen also have a neutron or two.

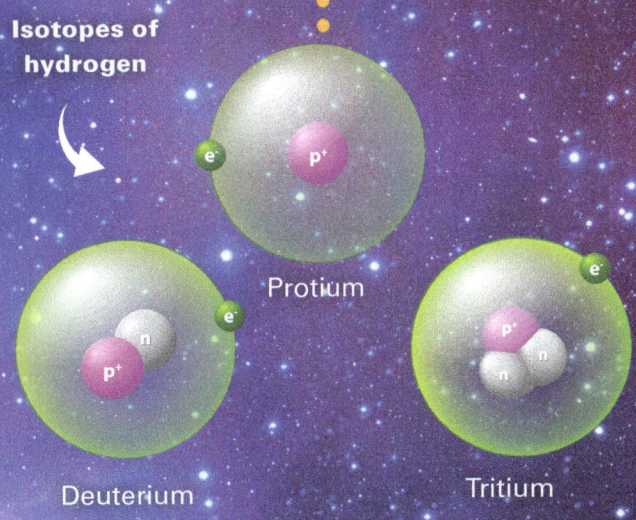

Isotopes of hydrogen

Protium
Deuterium
Tritium

These "primordial" hydrogen atoms were formed during the big bang, a cosmic explosion that scientists think started the expansion of the universe. Primordial hydrogen formed the first stars and gassy clouds called nebulas.

CAREER CORNER

Are you interested in the big bang and the origin of the universe? Become a cosmologist! Cosmologists use astronomy and particle physics to untangle the very beginnings of matter and the fundamental forces of the universe, such as gravity.

Heavy stuff!

Star-studded chemistry

Stellar lives

In nuclear fusion, two or more atomic nuclei *fuse* (combine) into a larger nucleus. This reaction releases an enormous amount of energy. Stars give off this energy through light and heat. The outward pressure of all that energy keeps stars from collapsing under their own gravity.

All stars begin by fusing hydrogen into helium—and that's how most stars spend most of their lives. In a star's core, hydrogen nuclei are squeezed together to form helium nuclei. Hydrogen-fusing stars are called *main sequence stars*. Astronomers estimate that some 90 percent of stars in the universe—including our sun—are main sequence stars.

TECH TIME

How do we know what a star is made of? We certainly can't travel to one and scoop up a sample! To learn a star's chemical makeup, astronomers use **spectroscopy**. Spectroscopy is the scientific study of how matter interacts with light and certain other forms of energy. In spectroscopy, scientists study the radiation given off, absorbed, or scattered by a material to learn more about the material's composition or structure. Because scientists know the wavelengths of light given off or absorbed by elements and **compounds** from laboratory experiments, they can break down the wavelengths given off by a body, such as a star or planet, to discover what it's made of.

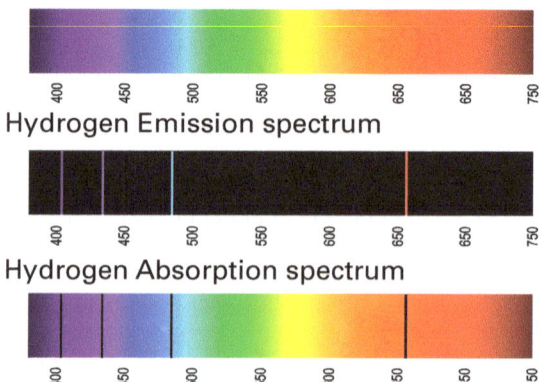

Why do the stars shine? Because of chemistry! Stars are colossal *nuclear fusion* reactors.

Main sequence fusion is slow and steady. A star the size of the sun can fuse hydrogen for 10 billion years before running out. Small stars called red dwarfs will be able to shine for trillions of years!

When stars like the sun run out of hydrogen fuel, they start to fuse helium into oxygen and carbon. This causes the star to balloon in size and cool into a red giant.

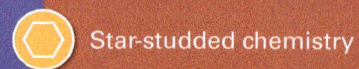

Star-studded chemistry

Vital element: helium

STATS

Symbol
He

Atomic Number
2

Atomic Mass
4.002602

Discoverer
Sir William Ramsay, Nils Langlet, P. T. Cleave

Helium is less dense than air, so balloons and other things filled with helium float! Unlike hydrogen gas, helium is not flammable. It can fill airships and children's balloons with no risk of combustion.

The largest industrial use of helium is in helium arc welding, sometimes called *heliarc* welding. The inert (nonreactive) helium keeps oxygen in the air from reaching the metal. If oxygen reaches the metal, it may cause the metal to burn or corrode. Helium is used to prevent certain substances from reacting chemically during storage, handling, and transportation.

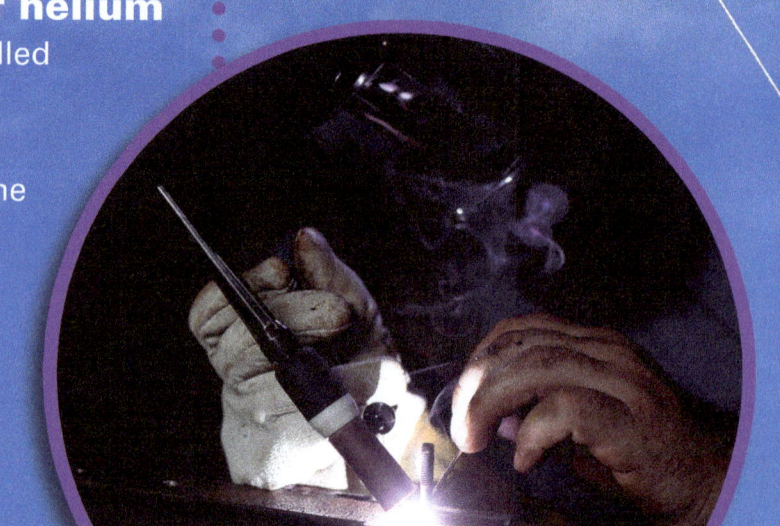

Helium, the most common product of stars, has many uses on Earth.

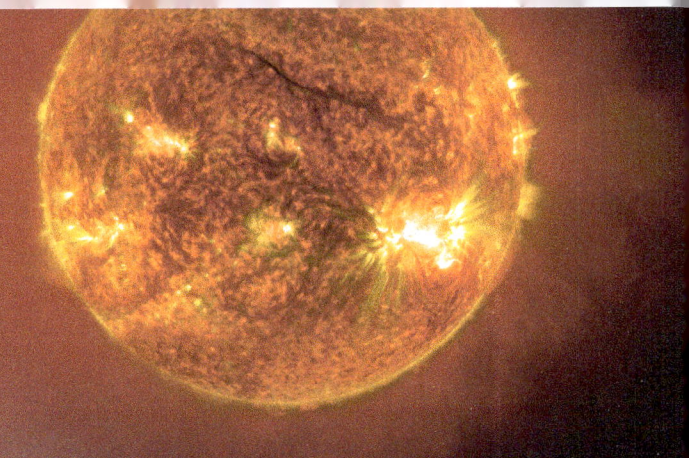

Liquid helium is one of the strangest of all liquids. Unlike most liquids, it conducts heat extremely well, it flows toward relatively warm places, and it expands instead of contracting when it cools. Liquid helium forms a film over everything it touches. This film can act as a siphon, carrying helium over the side of a container to a lower level. Weird!

DID YOU KNOW?

The name helium comes from the Greek word *helios*, meaning sun. Astronomers Pierre J. Janssen of France and Sir Joseph Lockyer of England detected helium in 1868 while observing the sun with one of the first spectroscopes.

Sunny days for chemical discovery!

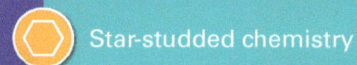Star-studded chemistry

Supergiants and supernovas

The sun seems huge. But there are other stars that are much bigger! So-called "high-mass" stars are at least eight times more massive than the sun. A high-mass star lives fast and dies young. The immense pressures in its core cause it to fuse all its hydrogen quickly—within about 10 million years. That's compared to the 10 billion years it will take our sun to burn though its hydrogen!

Sun

High-mass star

After using up its hydrogen, a high-mass star balloons in size—becoming 1,000 times the size of our sun. Such a high-mass star is called a supergiant. A supergiant fuses helium nuclei into carbon nuclei, and carbon nuclei to still heavier nuclei. However, each successive phase of fusion reaction lasts for less and less time. Eventually, a supergiant reaches iron. Fusing iron takes more energy than it produces. With no more energy coming from the core, the star collapses. The crushing pressures of the collapsing star fuse the iron in the core. This releases a cataclysmic blast of energy that tears through the inrushing layers and blows them into space—a supernova!

Our sun is on the puny side of the star scale. Other stars are far more massive. These stars produce more elements than do smaller stars. When one of the largest stars reaches the end of its life, it tears itself apart in a colossal explosion called a *supernova*.

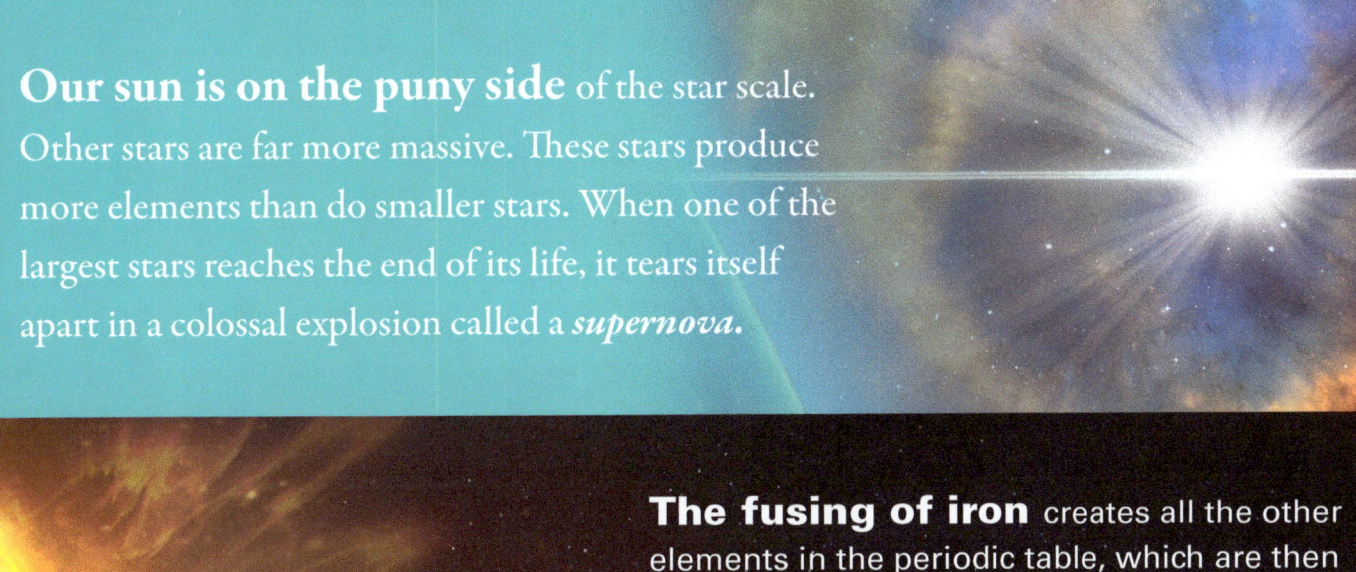

The fusing of iron creates all the other elements in the periodic table, which are then blown out into space through the supernova. Our solar system was seeded with these elements from ancient supernovas.

A supernova is an awe-inspiring sight. Supernovas bright enough to be seen with the naked eye often caught the notice of early civilizations. In 1054, Chinese astronomers recorded a supernova so bright that it was visible during the day. The explosion left behind a huge cloud of gas and dust now known as the **Crab Nebula**.

2

CLOSER TO HOME

Chemical reactions in our own solar system gave the planets and moons the characteristics they have today. We've learned much about the birth and development of our solar system—and our place in it—through studying its chemistry.

Our own star powers amazing chemical reactions throughout our solar system.

I'm a real Renaissance man!

The worlds of chemistry and astronomy have overlapped since the early history of science. The Danish scientist **Tycho Brahe** (1546-1601) is regarded as one of the finest astronomers of the pre-telescope era. His observations of the stars and planets were more precise than those of any earlier astronomer. But Brahe was also interested in alchemy, a way of studying and experimenting with matter that included elements of chemistry, philosophy, and spirituality. Brahe developed elixirs against plague containing coral, gold, and sapphire!

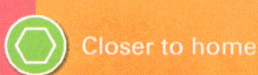 Closer to home

The windy sun

The solar wind is a continuous flow of *ionized* (charged) particles from the sun—electrons, protons, and some helium nuclei for good measure. It results chiefly from the expansion of gases in the corona, the outermost layer of the sun's *atmosphere*.

Earth's atmosphere is a thick soup compared to the solar wind. The solar wind has a density of about 82 ions per cubic inch (5 ions per cubic centimeter)—way, way less than the density of air on Earth. But, it flies from the sun at a breakneck speed—from 155 to 625 miles (250 to 1,000 kilometers) per second!

The high-speed particles push things away from the sun. For example, the *magnetosphere*, a region of strong magnetic forces surrounding Earth, is pushed into a teardrop shape by the solar wind as it streams past Earth.

When it comes to our solar system, the sun is the literal star of the show! Its influence is exerted not just by the light it produces but also by the stream of particles flowing from it, called the *solar wind*.

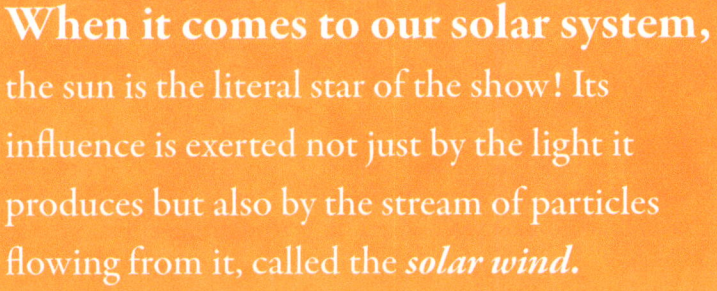

Mercury

The solar wind influences which planets can have atmospheres and what those atmospheres are made of. The wind strips away atoms and ions in a planet's upper atmosphere and blows them into space. The lightest elements, such as hydrogen and helium, rise to the top. Therefore, small, rocky planets either have an atmosphere made of heavier elements (like Earth's) or have no atmosphere at all, like Mercury.

It's too windy to hold on to an atmosphere!

TECH TIME

Can you sail on the solar wind? Yes! Engineers are designing special membranes called solar sails that can propel spacecraft. Because the solar wind has so few particles, these sails must be extremely large to capture as much of the solar wind as possible. The entire spacecraft must be lightweight to get anywhere in a reasonable amount of time. It's a technology for lightweight planetary probes, not solar yachts!

Closer to home

The moon rocks

The rocks that the Apollo astronauts brought home were remarkably similar to those of Earth's mantle. This similarity would be expected if Earth and the moon formed side by side. But, that idea couldn't explain why the moon was so much less dense than Earth. Analyses determined that the moon lacks the dense iron core that Earth has. If the moon formed alongside Earth, it should have the same density.

Moon rock

Earth rock

Hi, cousin!

With these ideas from chemical and physical analyses, scientists proposed the giant impact hypothesis. According to this idea, Earth collided with a planet-sized object, referred to as Theia, some 4.6 billion years ago. The impact caused a cloud of vaporized rock to shoot off Earth's surface and orbit the planet. The cloud cooled and condensed into a ring of small, solid bodies, which then gathered together, forming the moon.

The moon is Earth's companion in space, long a subject of fantasy and later a target for exploration. Scientists have achieved a better understanding of the moon than ever before in part by studying its chemistry.

See those dark blobs on the moon? They're called *maria*, Latin for *seas*. But, they're not liquid water, of course! They are made of a volcanic mineral called basalt, deposited in eruptions that peaked 3 billion years ago and occurred as recently as 1 billion years ago.

The eruptions might not be done! Scientists have found much smaller lava flows that occurred within the last 100 million years. It's possible the moon could still erupt today, but probably not enough to produce any new maria.

The **Apollo program**, which ran from 1961 to 1975, wasn't just a stunning feat of exploration. Daring Apollo astronauts also hauled 842 pounds (382 kilograms) of moon rocks back to Earth. These priceless pebbles have helped scientists to better understand the Earth-moon system.

Not sure how we're going to get this one back home…

19

Closer to home

Solar system snowballs

Comets are chunks of ice and rock from the outer reaches of the solar system. Scientists study comets to understand the chemistry of the solar system as it was forming 5 billion years ago.

Comets are famous for their tails. But how do they form? As a comet nears the inner solar system, heat from the sun vaporizes ice on the surface of its *nucleus* (core). The comet spews gas and dust particles into space, forming a cloud around the nucleus called the *coma*. Radiation from the sun pushes dust particles away from the coma, forming a tail called the dust tail. At the same time, the **solar wind** converts some of the comet's gases into charged particles called ions. They also stream away, forming an ion tail. Because comet tails are pushed by solar radiation and the solar wind, they always point away from the sun, no matter which direction the comet is going.

Our solar system isn't all planets and moons. It also includes bits of debris left over from their formation. The flashiest of these bits are icy bodies called comets.

What happens when a comet runs out of gas? Eventually, a comet will expel all its volatile materials. Such comets keep orbiting, but they emit no coma or tail as they near the sun. Astronomers call such bodies *extinct comets*.

DID YOU KNOW?

Visiting a comet? Better hold your nose! The volatile compounds of a comet—ammonia, sulfur dioxide, hydrogen cyanide, and hydrogen sulfide—are smelly and toxic. Ammonia is the chemical that gives urine its pungent smell. Hydrogen sulfide is the compound that makes the rotten-egg smell. Yuck!

Sorry, that was me…

Closer to home

Studying space rocks

Asteroids aren't your basic rocks. There are all kinds of them! Astronomers classify them according to their chemical composition. Most asteroids belong to one of three major types—C-type, S-type, and M-type.

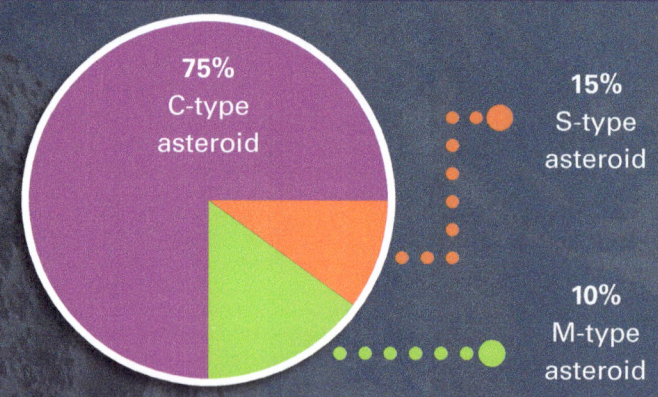

75% C-type asteroid

15% S-type asteroid

10% M-type asteroid

C-Type Asteroids

C-type asteroids make up about 75 percent of all known asteroids. They are rocky, with a chemical composition similar to that of the sun—minus the hydrogen and helium.

Roughly 15 percent are S-type asteroids. These asteroids are bright, rocky bodies that also contain some metal. The metal is an *alloy* of nickel and iron called nickel-iron. S-type asteroids consist of nickel-iron and silicates (rock-forming *compounds*) of iron and magnesium.

S-Type Asteroids

M-Type Asteroids

Most of the remaining asteroids belong to the third major group, the M-type asteroids. These bright objects consist of nearly pure nickel-iron. They may be fragments of the metallic core of a larger body that broke apart.

Asteroids may be less flashy than comets, but they also hold a wealth of chemical secrets.

Astronomers can learn all kinds of things about asteroids using Earthbound tools and orbital telescopes. But, there's no substitute for a physical examination. In 2018, NASA's probe OSIRIS-REx approached the asteroid Bennu, collected a sample, and returned it to Earth. The probe's name stands for "Origins, Spectral Interpretation, Resource Identification, Security, Regolith Explorer". The probe was designed to study the composition and properties of Bennu to learn more about the formation and evolution of the solar system. The sample of Bennu's surface was delivered to Earth in 2023. Scientists will continue studying it for generations!

 TECH TIME

Space technology companies are interested in mining asteroids for a resource that may surprise you—water! Some asteroids contain large amounts of the stuff. Why go for water instead of prospecting for precious metals? Water can be split into hydrogen and oxygen gas by passing an electric current through it. Hydrogen can be used as a spacecraft *propellant*. Oxygen can be used for astronauts to breathe. Harvesting these materials in space will enable spacecraft to fuel up in orbit around Earth or at other waypoints in the solar system, transforming space travel. Next stop: the stars!

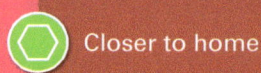

Impact-ful chemistry

Prehistoric reptiles ruled the planet. Then, a giant asteroid struck! And… nothing much changed. That's the story of the Manicouagan asteroid. Some 215 million years ago, early in the reign of the dinosaurs, an asteroid around 3 miles (5 kilometers) across slammed into what is now Quebec, Canada. Although the impact certainly caused widespread devastation, it just wasn't large enough to trigger a major extinction event. Life bounced back like nothing had happened. After eroding for millions of years, the impact crater gained a striking appearance in the 1960's. At that time, a hydroelectric dam flooded the crater's remnants, joining two modest rivers into a big, circular lake.

A larger impactor hitting a region with a particular chemical makeup, however, can create a worldwide disaster. At the end of the Cretaceous Period, about 66 million years ago, an asteroid about 6 miles (10 kilometers) in diameter collided with Earth. It struck a part of the seafloor that was thick with **hydrocarbons** and sulfur-containing **compounds**. The impact vaporized these compounds into soot and sulfates and blasted them into the **atmosphere,** where they blocked out the sun. Some studies estimate that the surface air temperature dropped by as many as 47 Fahrenheit degrees (26 Celsius degrees) for at least three years. Brr! The dramatic cooling devastated global ecosystems. Most plants died from the darkness and cold. Most animals starved or died of *hypothermia* (abnormally low body temperature).

As asteroids whizz around the solar system, they sometimes collide with planets—including Earth. Whether an asteroid causes terrible catastrophe or lands with a thud depends on its size and the chemistry of the area it strikes.

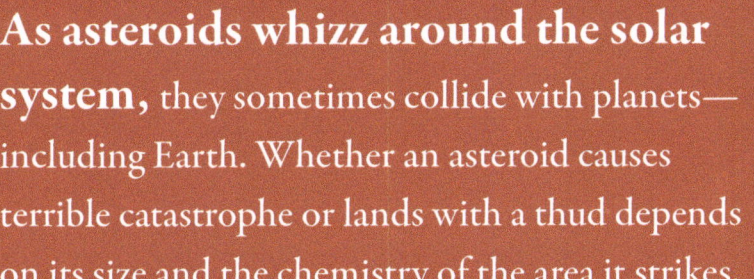

Scientists first detected the dinosaur-killing asteroid by the chemical signature it left all over Earth. On every continent, the layer between the Cretaceous and Paleogene periods contains large amounts of the chemical element iridium. Iridium is rare on Earth but common in asteroids. The band also contains pieces of shocked quartz. Shocked quartz is a variant of the mineral quartz in which the pieces have been exposed to extreme temperatures and pressures—such as those you'd expect to find in an asteroid impact.

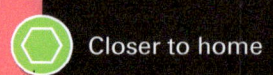

Gas giants

Jupiter is the largest, most massive planet in the solar system. It's made mostly of hydrogen and helium. Saturn is also made of hydrogen and helium. It's slightly smaller in size than Jupiter. But, Saturn has much less mass—only about a third that of Jupiter. How can this be, if it's made of the same stuff? Hydrogen and helium are highly compressible. That means they are easily squeezed to a greater density. The greater mass of Jupiter squeezes the hydrogen and helium much more strongly than does the mass of Saturn, leading to Jupiter's greater density.

DID YOU KNOW?

If you're ever in the outer solar system and need to cool your drink, swing by Saturn! The planet's rings are 98 percent water ice, most in chunks no larger than a boulder. However, there's also some rock and dust mixed in, giving the rings their grey color. So pick your ice carefully!

We're so cool!

The four outer planets of the solar system are made of gas. These huge planets are massive enough to hold onto their hydrogen and helium in the face of the *solar wind*.

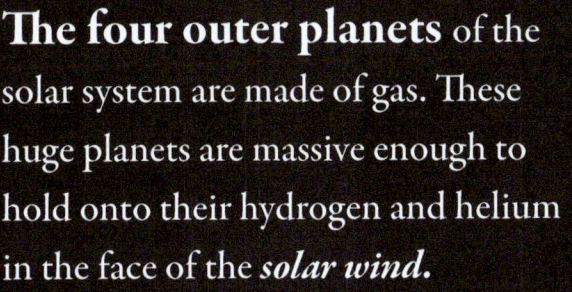

The outermost two planets are nicknamed ice giants for their chilly temperatures and the presence of ice crystals in their swirling clouds. Methane ice crystals in Uranus's *atmosphere* give the planet its pale blue-green color. Neptune gets its bluish color from traces of ammonia in its atmosphere.

Neptune

Uranus

Closer to home

Looking for life

All living things on Earth need water to survive. Therefore, water is the first thing astronomers look for in a potentially habitable body—that is, one capable of supporting life. In fact, a star's habitable zone is defined as the region around it in which liquid water could exist on the surface of an orbiting planet. Earth is smack-dab in the middle of our sun's habitable zone.

The Fishing Cone hot spring in Yellowstone National Park, Wyoming

Europa, a moon of Jupiter

Hydrothermal vents

Recent analyses of smaller bodies in our solar system have upended the concept of the habitable zone. They have shown that many bodies beyond the habitable zone may possess oceans of liquid water beneath a crust of rock or ice. On such bodies, hydrothermal vents like those at the bottom of Earth's oceans could host communities of living things in total darkness. A collection of moons of Saturn and Jupiter, the giant asteroid Ceres, and even Pluto are all now suspected of containing liquid water under their surfaces.

One of the most compelling reasons to explore the solar system is to answer the question of how rare life is.

The presence of water alone isn't enough to prove life exists somewhere. *Biosignatures* are signs created by the presence or activity of living things. Often, these are chemical compounds that can't easily form without living things. Many are compounds that usually break down or react with other compounds quickly, so they need constant replenishment to remain in an *atmosphere*.

CAREER CORNER

Love studying the planets, moons, and stars? You can be an astronomer! Astronomy involves many branches of science—astronomers use chemistry in the analysis of stars, nebula, and planets.

Closer to home

Earth's evil twin

You've heard of the *greenhouse effect*, in which carbon dioxide and other gases in the *atmosphere* trap heat from the sun? On Earth, carbon dioxide makes up a little over 0.004 percent of the atmosphere. For every 1 billion *molecules* in the atmosphere, you'd get about four of CO_2. But on Venus, carbon dioxide makes up a whopping 96 percent of the atmosphere! That cranks up the greenhouse effect to extreme levels, causing the planet to swelter at 870 °F (465 °C)! The thick atmosphere also produces crushing pressures at the surface.

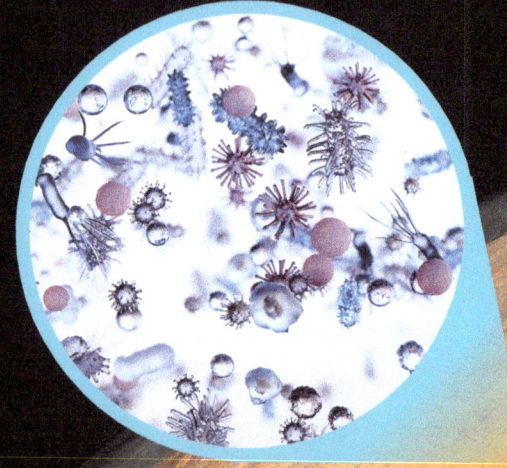

The extreme conditions on Venus's surface make it impossible for life to exist there. But up in the clouds, conditions are much more hospitable. About 30 miles (50 kilometers) up, temperatures and pressures are similar to those on Earth's surface. This fact has led some scientists to speculate that microbes could float in Venus's clouds.

In 2020, researchers were surprised to detect the *molecule* phosphine in the clouds of Venus. Phosphine is an atom of phosphorus bonded to three atoms of hydrogen (PH_3). On Earth, microbes in *anaerobic* (oxygen-free) environments produce phosphine. Phosphine is also very reactive, meaning it combines easily with other molecules. That means it must be continuously replenished for it to exist in an atmosphere. The most common way phosphine gets into Earth's atmosphere is through the action of microbes.

Phosphine (PH_3)

Venus's swirling clouds mesmerized the first people to observe the planet with a telescope. Even though we know more about the planet today, many mysteries remain hidden.

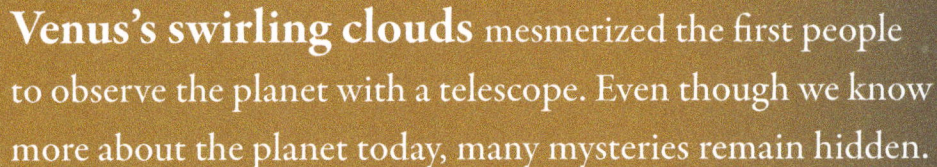

Further studies in 2024 found ammonia in Venus's atmosphere. This molecule consists of a nitrogen atom bonded to three hydrogen atoms (NH_3). Venus's clouds possess huge amounts of sulfuric acid, making it too acidic for even the most extreme microbes on Earth. But ammonia in the clouds would lower the acidity. The researchers speculate that living things could be releasing the ammonia to make their cloudy homes comfier.

Ammonia (NH_3)

These discoveries are interesting but nothing close to proof of life on Venus! Further study and sampling are needed to puzzle out our neighbor planet's strange chemistry.

Closer to home

The Red Planet

Astronomers are fascinated by Mars because, billions of years ago, it was much like Earth. It even had liquid water on its surface. How can we tell? First, there is physical evidence all over the planet, including deltas, riverbeds, and lakebeds left behind by ancient waters. However, there's also chemical evidence in the rocks. Ice is present near the Martian surface and in greater quantities at the poles. Robotic rovers have found hydrated (water-containing) minerals at these sites.

The clear evidence of liquid water on Mars's surface in the past has made it a prime target in the search for life—either in the planet's ancient past or still living today. In 2024, NASA's Perseverance rover found a rock nicknamed "Cheyava Falls" that shows all the ingredients necessary to host ancient life. Whitish bands of calcium sulfate running through the rock indicate that it was once permeated with water. Between these bands, Perseverance detected the presence of organic *molecules*. In this area, scientists also noted "leopard spots" where chemical reactions occurred that could have provided fuel for microbial life.

Mars is a barren wasteland today. But, its chemistry shows that it once had all the ingredients necessary to support life. Whether life ever took hold there remains one of the great mysteries of the solar system.

Since NASA's Curiosity rover landed in 2012, it has been detecting unusual spikes in atmospheric methane, a possible *biosignature*. Methane is a *hydrocarbon* consisting of an atom of carbon bonded to four hydrogen atoms. It is extremely reactive, so something must be replacing it in the *atmosphere*. On Earth, methane in the atmosphere is produced by microbes.

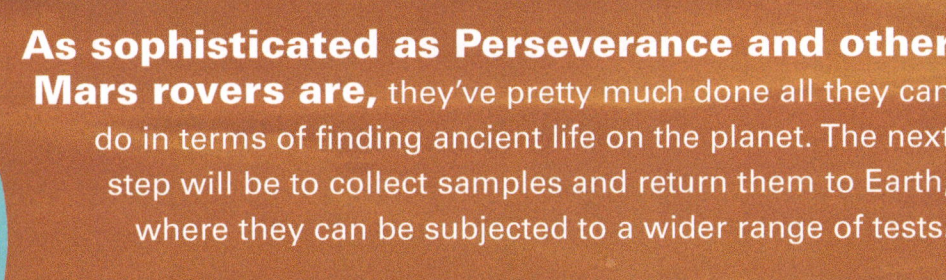

As sophisticated as Perseverance and other Mars rovers are, they've pretty much done all they can do in terms of finding ancient life on the planet. The next step will be to collect samples and return them to Earth, where they can be subjected to a wider range of tests.

The first landers to reach Mars were **NASA's Viking landers,** which both touched down in 1976. The landers took the first close-up pictures of the Martian surface and analyzed the soil. They found no strong evidence for life, but astronomers haven't given up the hunt!

Closer to home

Titan-ic chemistry

- **Atmospheres are usually the property of planets,** but the mighty moon Titan has one of the thickest atmospheres in the solar system. Like Earth's atmosphere, Titan's consists mostly of nitrogen gas. But, the similarities stop there. Such **hydrocarbons** as methane make up the rest of Titan's atmosphere.

Titan

The methane condenses into clouds and rains down on Titan's surface! When the lander Huygens parachuted to the surface in 2005, it showed rocks weathered by erosion from methane rains and flows.

Titan, the largest moon of Saturn, could easily be mistaken for an alien planet. It's larger than Mercury, possesses a thick, swirling *atmosphere,* and has a surface dotted with strange lakes.

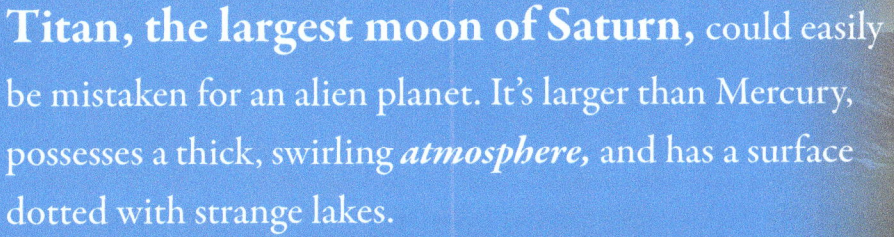

Images from Huygens's parent craft, the space probe Cassini, showed that Titan's north pole is dotted with huge lakes of methane and ethane. Such hydrocarbons are only liquid at frigid temperatures. Titan's surface is about −290 °F (−179 °C)! These temperatures can support *cryovolcanism,* a form of volcanic activity in which water ice acts like rock and liquid water like lava! Researchers have identified regions where fissures spew liquid water onto Titan's surface.

TECH TIME

Titan's atmosphere is so thick that it's easier to fly there than on Earth! NASA plans to take advantage of this fact with its Dragonfly probe. Planned for a 2028 launch, the probe will use several propellers to fly around the surface of Titan—just like a drone on Earth.

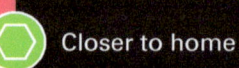
Closer to home

Frozen worlds

Pluto lurks in the Kuiper belt, a group of icy bodies at the edge of the solar system. When NASA's New Horizons probe flew by Pluto in 2016, it revealed a surprisingly active world covered in various ices and frosts. The area around Pluto's equator is dark red. It is made up of water ice and of methane frost that has been broken down by solar radiation. This dark belt is broken by a bright, heart-shaped basin composed of methane ice, nitrogen ice, and frozen carbon monoxide. Other areas on Pluto appear reddish-brown and are covered with frozen methane.

The brightest regions of Pluto have no visible craters and are younger than 10 million years old. Any large craters there were erased by flowing ices, likely through *cryovolcanism*.

Pluto is the most famous resident of the outer reaches of the solar system. But the dwarf planet has a secret twin: Triton, a moon of Neptune!

Astronomers think that Triton used to orbit the sun in the Kuiper belt as well, until gravitational fluctuations resulted in Neptune capturing the dwarf planet. One of the reasons for this suspicion is that Triton orbits in the opposite direction from that in which Neptune spins. A moon that forms alongside a planet tends to orbit in the same direction the planet rotates.

In 1989, NASA's probe Voyager 2 photographed geyserlike plumes 5 miles (8 kilometers) high erupting from Triton's surface. These eruptions were likely produced by icy cryovolcanoes!

DID YOU KNOW?

Could life exist at the edge of the solar system? Pluto and Triton are thought to have oceans of liquid water beneath their surfaces. Furthermore, the geysers erupting from Triton show that its ocean could have hydrothermal vents that could provide a source of energy for living things. Scientists and engineers have developed missions to fly to Triton and sample the plumes from its geysers, but the vast distance has kept their proposals on the drawing board.

EXPLORING SPACE

To get a rocket into space requires precision engineering and incredible amounts of energy. Engineers must understand the chemistry of the materials used in building the rocket as well as the chemistry of the *propellants*.

We can only learn so much with Earthbound tools. We must go to space to more fully study the planets, moons, and asteroids. It takes a firm grasp of chemistry to get there.

Getting humans into space and keeping them alive there is even harder. Humans need a constant supply of oxygen, water, and food to survive. We release a variety of waste products that have to be dealt with. Engineers are getting better at supporting life in space, but there's still a long way to go before we can create self-sufficient settlements on the moon and Mars.

One of the first rocket scientists was the American scientist **Robert Goddard.** He became interested in rockets while in college. He tested the first liquid-fueled rocket in 1926. His hot-rod rockets guzzled gasoline!

More pickup than a V8!

Exploring space

Getting to space

Even the fastest airplanes can't make it to space. Jet engines use oxygen from the atmosphere to combust their fuel. Higher up, as the atmosphere gets thinner, jet engines get less efficient. What if you bring along your own oxygen? That's the idea behind the rocket! A rocket is a type of engine that pushes itself forward or upward by producing thrust. A rocket engine uses only the substances carried within it. As a result, a rocket can operate in outer space, where there is no air.

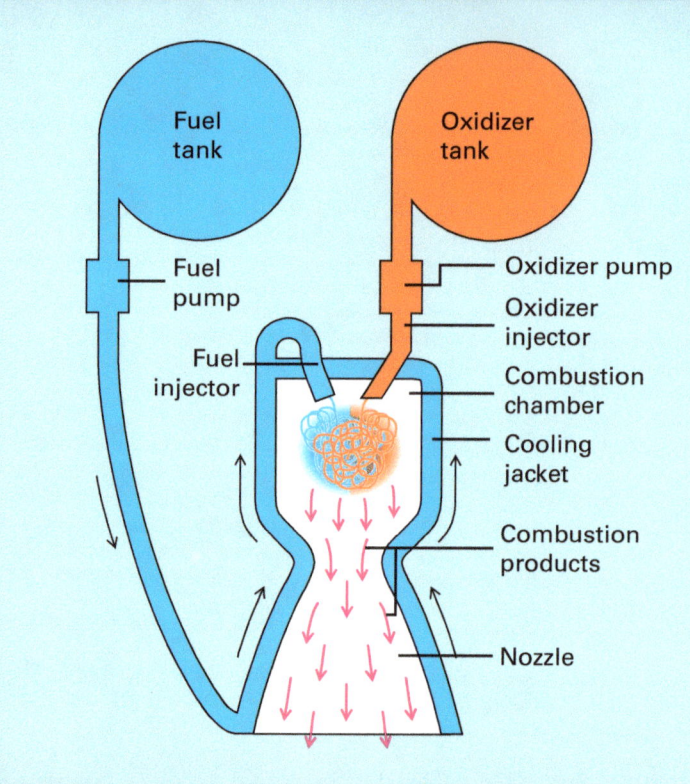

Like a jet engine or even a conventional automobile engine, a rocket engine makes use of the chemical reaction of *combustion*. But instead of burning fuel in air, a rocket mixes an oxidizer with its fuel. The oxidizer provides the oxygen atoms for the reaction. The chemistry of oxidizers varies, but an oxidizer can be as simple as liquified oxygen gas. An oxidizer can combust fuel more rapidly than air, and a rocket engine doesn't require major moving parts, such as a turbine, enabling a rocket engine to be more powerful than a jet engine.

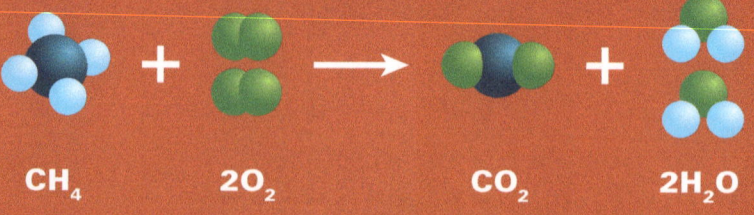

$CH_4 \quad + \quad 2O_2 \quad \rightarrow \quad CO_2 \quad + \quad 2H_2O$

We've learned so much about the cosmos with ground-based telescopes and other instruments. But, there is so much more that can be done outside of Earth's *atmosphere*. Rocket engines help us get there!

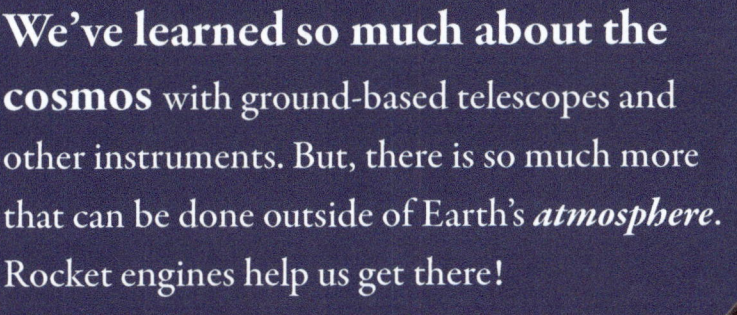

When maneuvering toward a space station, you don't want to worry about your control thrusters failing to start. So, such thrusters often use hypergols, *propellants* that ignite when the fuel and oxidizer mix. They don't require an ignition system; they just work! But, they don't pack as much power as standard propellants.

The launch of Gemini 12 on November 11th, 1966. The thrusters on the Gemini-Titan II rocket used hypergols.

Hypergols are also naturally extremely volatile. Hypergol explosions have caused some of the worst ground accidents in the history of rocketry! Hypergols are therefore no longer commonly used for the first stages of rockets, in which safety and power are more important than the assurance of ignition. Common hypergols include the fuel hydrazine (N_2H_4) and the oxidizer nitrogen tetroxide (N_2O_4).

Loading rocket fuel

41

Exploring space

Living in space

Humans take in oxygen and breathe out carbon dioxide (CO_2). Carbon dioxide is toxic at high concentrations, so it must be scrubbed from the cabins of spacecraft. Scrubbing devices combine lithium hydroxide (LiOH) with carbon dioxide to form lithium carbonate (Li_2CO_3) and water (H_2O).

Chemical scrubbers eventually get saturated with CO_2 and must be replaced. What if you could just filter out the carbon dioxide like dust with an air filter? It's possible with zeolite filters. Zeolite is any of a group of crystalline mineral *compounds* whose framework of atoms forms microscopic tunnels and "rooms." The internal structure of zeolites makes them useful as filters. Nitrogen and oxygen gas *molecules* can pass through, but water vapor and carbon dioxide get trapped inside. On the International Space Station (ISS), zeolite filters collect water vapor and carbon dioxide. After a time, the filter is exposed to an adsorption layer to remove the water vapor for recycling. Then, the filter is exposed to the vacuum of space, allowing the collected CO_2 to float away!

Humans have more needs than spacecraft. Allowing people to safely live and work in space requires plenty of chemistry.

Each astronaut uses about 1 gallon (4 liters) of water per day for drinking, food preparation, and washing. Imagine if a cargo vessel had to fly some 200 gallons (800 liters) of water to the ISS each month! Instead, engineers have developed ways to recycle all the water that they can—including urine! Urine is about 95 percent water, but it also contains urea, creatinine, uric acid, and salts. Aboard the ISS, a two-phase filtration process recovers almost 98 percent of the water from urine! The recovered water, along with water recovered from the air with dehumidifiers, goes through an extensive filtration process before it is again used by astronauts.

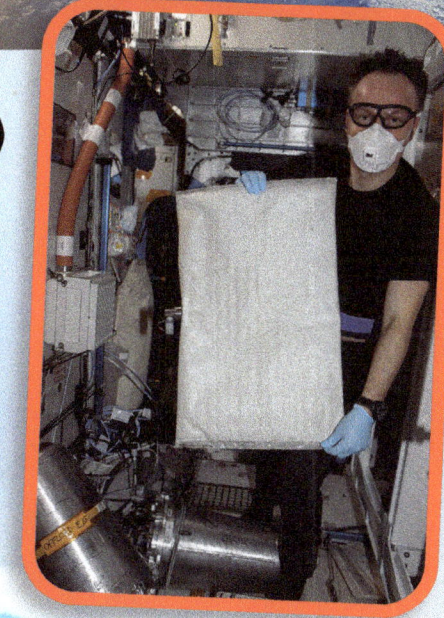

TECH TIME

Astronauts aboard the ISS are still under the protection of Earth's *magnetosphere*. This magnetic "shell" around the planet keeps away much of the harmful radiation from the sun and outer space. If astronauts are to ever stay on the moon for extended periods or visit Mars, they will have to be protected from the high levels of radiation there. One material that might help is hydrogenated boron nitride nanotubes (BNNT's). In BNNT's, atoms of boron and carbon bond to form long, hollow tubes with a single-atom thickness. Adding hydrogen to bond to the boron and nitrogen atoms improves their radiation-blocking abilities. The material is also strong enough to be used for structural components! Engineers envision placing long strands of hydrogenated BNNT's into a mold along with a binding agent to form spacecraft parts—similar to the process used to make carbon fiber or fiberglass.

Build a rocket

What you'll need:
- Baking soda
- Plastic 2-liter soda bottle
- 3 pencils or chopsticks
- Vinegar
- Paper towel
- Cork that fits the mouth of the 2-liter bottle
- Tape
- Construction paper and coloring supplies (optional)
- Safety glasses

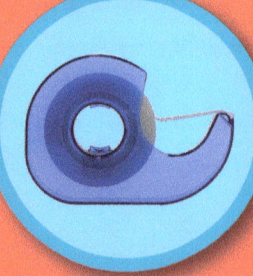

Give it a try

1. Tape the three pencils to the bottle so that the bottle will balance on them with the mouth of the bottle about an inch or so (3 centimeters) from the ground. These are the rocket's landing legs.
2. If you wish, decorate your rocket with construction paper, and add fins and a nose cone.
3. Take the rocket outside and fill half of the bottle with vinegar.
4. Pour about 3 tablespoons (50 grams) of baking soda in a paper towel and roll it tightly.
5. Place the rolled paper towel into the bottle and seal the mouth with the cork.
6. Quickly set the rocket down on its landing legs on a flat surface and back away.
7. After a short while, your rocket should launch into the sky!

Now that you've learned about chemistry in space, let's build a rocket! It won't get into orbit, but it shows how chemistry and physics interact in real rockets. It's also a lot of fun!

Try this next!

Now that you know how to make a baking soda bottle rocket, experiment! Use a stopwatch to measure how long your rocket stays in the air. Adjust your rocket design to go even higher by adjusting the propellant mix, nozzle shape, and body design. You're a rocket scientist now!

QUESTION TIME!

What does your best design look like? Why do you think it works? What are the similarities between your rocket and a conventional rocket? What are the differences? If you love designing rockets, look up model rocketry (with a parent's approval) and take your skills to the next level!

Index

A
alloys, 22
Apollo program, 18-19
asteroids, 22-25, 28
astronomy (career), 29
atoms, 6-8, 17, 30-31, 33, 40, 42-43
atmospheres, 16-17, 24, 27, 29-31, 33-35, 40

B
Bennu (asteroid), 23
biosignatures, 29, 33
boron nitride nanotubes (BNNT's), 43
Brahe, Tycho, 15

C
carbon dioxide, 30, 42
Cassini (space probe), 35
Ceres (asteroid), 28
Cleave, P. T., 10
combustion, 40
comets, 20-21
compounds, 9, 21-22, 24, 29, 42
cosmology (career), 7
Crab Nebula, 13
cryovolcanism, 35-37
Curiosity (Mars rover), 33

D
Dragonfly probe, 35

G
Goddard, Robert, 39
greenhouse effect, 30

H
helium, 8-12, 16-17, 26-27
Huygens lander, 34-35
hydrocarbons, 24, 33-35
hydrogen, 6-9, 12, 17, 23, 26-27, 30-31, 33, 43
hypergols, 41

I
International Space Station (ISS), 42-43
ions, 16-17, 20
iridium, 25
iron, 12-13, 18, 22
isotopes, 7

J
Janssen, Pierre J., 11
Jupiter, 26, 28

K
Kuiper belt, 36-37

L
Langlet, Nils, 10
life on other worlds, search for, 28-33, 37
Lockyer, Sir Joseph, 11

M
magnetospheres, 16, 43
Mars, 32-33, 39, 43
Mercury, 17, 35
methane, 27, 33-36
molecules, 30-32, 42
moon, of Earth, 18-19, 39, 43

N
National Aeronautics and Space Administration (NASA), 23, 32-33, 35-37
Neptune, 27, 37
New Horizons (space probe), 36
nickel-iron, 22
nuclear fusion, 8-9, 12-13

O
oceans, on other worlds, 28, 37
OSIRIS-REx (space probe), 23
oxygen, 9-10, 23, 39-40, 42

P
Perseverance (Mars rover), 32-33
Pluto, 28, 36-37

propellants, 23, 38, 41

R
Ramsay, Sir William, 10
rockets, 38-43

S
Saturn, 26-28
solar sails, 17
solar wind, 16-17, 20, 27
spectroscopy, 9, 11
sun, 11-13, 16-17, 20, 24, 28, 43
supergiant stars, 12-13
supernovas, 12-13

T
Titan (moon of Saturn), 34-35
Triton (moon of Neptune), 37

U
Uranus, 27

V
Venus, 30-31
Viking landers, 33
Voyager 2 (space probe), 37

Z
zeolite, 42

Glossary

alloy (AL oy)—a mixture of a metal and at least one other element

atmosphere (AT muh sfihr)—the mass of gases that surrounds a planet or moon

biosignature (BY oh SIHG nuh chuhr)—a sign created by the presence or activity of living things

combustion (kuhm BUHS chuhn)—a chemical reaction that gives off heat and light. Combustion involves the rapid combination of oxygen with a fuel to produce burning.

compound (KOM pownd)—a substance that contains more than one kind of atom

cryovolcanism (KRY oh VOL kuh nihz uhm)—geologic activity on planets and moons in which liquid water erupts out of the ground and hardens into ice, similar to volcanic eruptions on Earth

greenhouse effect (GREEN HOWS uh FEHKT)—a process that traps heat in Earth's or some other planet's atmosphere, causing the surface temperature to rise

hydrocarbon (HY droh KAHR buhn)—a chemical compound containing hydrogen and oxygen

ion (EYE uhn)—an atom or molecule that has an electric charge. Such a particle is said to be ionized.

isotope (EYE suh tohp)—one of two or more atoms of the same chemical element that differ in the amount of matter they contain. Isotopes of the same chemical element have different atomic masses.

magnetosphere (mag NEE tuh sfihr)—the region of space near a planet that is dominated by its magnetic field

molecule (MOL uh kyool)—the smallest particle into which a substance can be divided and still have the chemical identity of the original substance

nuclear fusion (NOO klee uhr FYOO zhuhn)—the combining of two atomic nuclei to form the nucleus of a heavier element

propellant (pruh PEHL uhnt)—solid or liquid fuel that is turned into gas and put under pressure to push a spacecraft forward

solar wind (SOH luhr wihnd)—the continuous flow of particles from the sun

spectroscopy (spehk TROS kuh pee)—the scientific study of how matter interacts with light and certain other forms of energy.
supernova (soo puhr NOH vuh)—an exploding star that can become billions of times as bright as the sun before gradually fading from view

www.ingramcontent.com/pod-product-compliance
Lightning Source LLC
Chambersburg PA
CBHW061251170426
43191CB00041B/2411